WEYBRIDGE

JEAN SMITH has lived in Weybridge for over 40 years. As part of an Open University degree she became involved in local history research and joined the Walton and Weybridge Local History Society, recently completing 10 years as Chairman. She is Secretary of the Friends of Elmbridge Museum, where she works as a volunteer answering local history queries.

The Church 1904 51692

WEYBRIDGE

JEAN SMITH

FRANCIS FRITH'S
TOWN & CITY
MEMORIES

First published as Weybridge, Living Memories of Your Town
in 2001 by Black Horse Books, an imprint of The Francis Frith Collection®
Revised edition published in the United Kingdom in 2005 by
The Francis Frith Collection as Weybridge, Town and City Memories

Limited Hardback Edition 2005 ISBN 1-84589-063-9

Paperback Edition 2005 ISBN 1-85937-991-5

Text and Design copyright © The Francis Frith Collection®
Photographs copyright © The Francis Frith Collection®
except where indicated

The Frith® photographs and the Frith® logo are reproduced under licence from
Heritage Photographic Resources Ltd, the owners of the Frith® archive and trademarks.
'The Francis Frith Collection', 'Francis Frith' and 'Frith' are registered trademarks of Heritage
Photographic Resources Ltd.

All rights reserved. No photograph in this publication may be sold to a third party other
than in the original form of this publication, or framed for sale to a third party.
No parts of this publication may be reproduced, stored in a retrieval system, or transmitted,
in any form, or by any means, electronic, mechanical, photocopying, recording or otherwise,
without the prior permission of the publishers and copyright holder

British Library Cataloguing in Publication Data

Weybridge
Town and City Memories
Jean Smith

The Francis Frith Collection®
Frith's Barn, Teffont,
Salisbury, Wiltshire SP3 5QP
Tel: +44 (0) 1722 716 376
Email: info@francisfrith.co.uk
www.francisfrith.co.uk

Aerial photographs reproduced under licence from Simmons Aerofilms Limited
Historical Ordnance Survey maps reproduced under licence from Homecheck.co.uk

Printed and bound in England

Front Cover: **WEYBRIDGE, BAKER STREET 1903** 49902t
The colour-tinting in this image is for illustrative purposes only,
and is not intended to be historically accurate

Every attempt has been made to contact copyright holders of illustrative material.
We will be happy to give full acknowledgement in future editions for any items not
credited. Any information should be directed to The Francis Frith Collection.

AS WITH ANY HISTORICAL DATABASE, THE FRANCIS FRITH ARCHIVE IS CONSTANTLY BEING
CORRECTED AND IMPROVED, AND THE PUBLISHERS WOULD WELCOME INFORMATION ON
OMISSIONS OR INACCURACIES

FRANCIS FRITH'S
Town & City
MEMORIES

Contents

The Making of an Archive	6
Weybridge from the air	8
Introduction	10
The Thames	12
Ordnance Survey Map	26
Thames to Town	28
The Town Centre	40
Towards the Heath	50
Surrey County Map	62
Upper Weybridge	64
Names of Subscribers	86
Index	87

VOUCHER FOR FREE MOUNTED PRINT   91

The Making of an Archive

Francis Frith, Victorian founder of the world-famous photographic archive, was a devout Quaker and a highly successful Victorian businessman. By 1860 he was already a multi-millionaire, having established and sold a wholesale grocery business in Liverpool. He had also made a series of pioneering photographic journeys to the Nile region. The images he returned with were the talk of London. An eminent modern historian has likened their impact on the population of the time to that on our own generation of the first photographs taken on the surface of the moon.

Frith had a passion for landscape, and was as equally inspired by the countryside of Britain as he was by the desert regions of the Nile. He resolved to set out on a new career and to use his skills with a camera. He established a business in Reigate as a specialist publisher of topographical photographs.

Frith lived in an era of immense and sometimes violent change. For the poor in the early part of Victoria's reign work was a drudge and the hours long, and ordinary people had precious little free time. Most had not travelled far beyond the boundaries of their own town or village. Mass tourism was in its infancy during the 1860s, but during the next decade the railway network and the establishment of Bank Holidays and half-Saturdays gradually made it possible for the working man and his family to enjoy holidays and to see a little more of the world. With characteristic business acumen, Francis Frith foresaw that these new tourists would enjoy having souvenirs to commemorate their days out. He began selling photo-souvenirs of seaside resorts and beauty spots, which the Victorian public pasted into treasured family albums.

Frith's aim was to photograph every town and village in Britain. For the next thirty years he travelled the country by train and by pony and trap, producing fine photographs of seaside resorts and beauty spots that were keenly bought by millions of Victorians.

The Rise of Frith & Co

Each photograph was taken with tourism in mind, the small team of Frith photographers concentrating on busy shopping streets, beaches, seafronts, picturesque lanes and villages. They also photographed buildings: the Victorian and Edwardian eras were times of huge building activity, and town halls, libraries, post offices, schools and technical colleges were springing up all over the country. They were invariably celebrated by a proud Victorian public, and photo souvenirs – visual records – published by F Frith & Co were sold in their hundreds of thousands. In addition, many new commercial buildings such as hotels, inns and pubs were photographed, often because their owners specifically commissioned Frith postcards or prints of them for re-sale or for publicity purposes.

In order to gain some understanding of the scale of Frith's business one only has to look at the catalogue issued by Frith & Co in 1886: it runs to some 670 pages. By 1890 Frith had created the greatest specialist photographic publishing company in the world, with over 2,000 stockists! The picture on the right shows the Frith & Co display board on the wall of the stockist at Ingleton in the Yorkshire Dales (left of window). Beautifully constructed with a mahogany frame and gilt inserts, it displayed a dozen scenes.

The Making of an Archive

Postcard Bonanza

The ever-popular holiday postcard we know today took many years to appear, and F Frith & Co was in the vanguard of its development. Postcards became a hugely popular means of communication and sold in their millions. Frith's company took full advantage of this boom and soon became the major publisher of photographic view postcards.

Francis Frith died in 1898 at his villa in Cannes, his great project still growing. His sons Eustace and Cyril continued their father's monumental task, expanding the number of views offered to the public and recording more and more places in Britain, as the coasts and countryside were opened up to mass travel. The archive Frith created continued in business for another seventy years. By 1970 it contained over a third of a million pictures of 7,000 cities, towns and villages. The massive photographic record Frith has left to us stands as a living monument to a special and very remarkable man.

This book shows Weybridge as it was photographed by this world-famous archive at various periods in its development over the past 150 years. Every photograph was taken for a specific commercial purpose, which explains why the selection may not show every aspect of the town landscape. However, the photographs, compiled from one of the world's most celebrated archives, provide an important and absorbing record of your town.

From the Air

Weybridge from the Air 1964 AFA128355

WEYBRIDGE FROM THE AIR

Introduction

Weybridge is a small town, 19 miles from London, situated where the River Wey enters the Thames at its most southerly point. From medieval times there has been a bridge of some sort across the Wey, hence the name of the town, but no bridge across the Thames.

Weybridge remained a small and insignificant village until Henry VIII decided to build one of his many palaces at Oatlands in 1538. The Oatlands estate covered the village and a vast area of surrounding countryside to provide adequate hunting of deer for the court. This continued with succeeding monarchs until the execution of Charles I in 1649, after which Crown property was seized by Parliament and sold. Oatlands Palace was demolished by its new owner, Robert Turbridge, and the materials sold.

Large estates, especially Oatlands and Portmore Park, continued to dominate the village, and important figures, many of them naval, owned them. Royalty was represented in the person of the Duke of York, second son of George III, who owned Oatlands House from 1788 to 1824. Small shops opened to meet their needs, and cottages were built to accommodate their servants, such as gardeners and bailiffs.

The coming of the London and Southampton Railway in 1838 opened up Weybridge to new residents; these were professional and wealthy people who worked in the City, but wanted their families to live in the country. Large houses were built on the Heath near the station from the 1840s. Trains to London conveyed passengers, but were also able to take their horses and carriages up to the 1870s. The

Introduction

THE CHURCH AND THE RIVER 1890 23586

This view displays the rural character of Weybridge at the end of the 19th century. The River Wey flows from right to left towards its confluence with the Thames half a mile further downstream. The bridge, built in 1865, carries the main road to Chertsey. Behind it is Grove House, later renamed Bridge House, typical of the many large houses in the area. The spire of the parish church of St James, sometimes called the Cathedral of the Thames Valley, is in the background.

advantage of the railway to 19th-century commuters was indicated in the number of properties being advertised for sale as early as 1864. The downside of this was the increasing number of house burglaries; the Surrey Advertiser commented that this was due to the easy access from London by train. As more large houses were built, so were supporting cottages and shops in the centre of the village. The increased population led to the building of a larger parish church in 1848.

Later, the break-up of the large estates in the 1880s and 1890s led to the further development of the town centre with houses for artisans and clerical workers. The commercial part of the town catered for this new population, and the development of the motor-car quickly resulted in the arrival of garages and service stations as early as 1903. This feature was encouraged by the building of the first motor-car racing track at Brooklands by Hugh Locke King, which opened in 1907.

Between the wars Council housing was built under new government legislation; the council estates covered fields previously grazed by cattle. This continued after the last war with housing for Vickers-Armstong Aircraft factory workers. Today, the industries have been replaced by large offices belonging to multi-national companies, while the attractiveness of the area and its nearness to London brings employees of many nationalities to buy and rent properties.

The Thames

The River 1900 49910

This peaceful river scene was taken where the Wey joins the River Thames. Ahead is the weir for Shepperton Lock, and to the left are boats for hire. The boatman is skilfully using a pole to manoeuvre the punt.

The River Thames has always been an attractive and important feature of Weybridge life. Its confluence with the River Wey was important for the transport of goods to and from London from early times, but the improvement of the River Wey in 1653 increased the amount of traffic using the waterways. This early river scheme was designed to improve the navigation of the winding River Wey by cutting channels and installing locks between the Thames and Guildford, later extended to Godalming. This made easier the transport of agricultural goods, including grain, and associated commodities like timber, chalk and lime to London. Return cargoes included coal and manufactured goods. An unusual commodity was gunpowder from the mills at Chilworth, and the safety aspects of transferring and storing this at Weybridge for onwards transport to London caused the local vestry much concern.

By the end of the 19th century, however, the use of the Thames for pleasure and relaxation was increasing. The regattas were major social events, and the availability of punts and skiffs, or larger launches for hire, created employment on the river banks for boatbuilders. The locks on the Thames were large enough to take sizeable vessels, so this became the heyday of Salter's Steamers and other boat firms. The leisure aspect of the Thames is shown in the 1890 view from the Lincoln Arms Hotel (23589, right), which also shows the rural nature of the area despite its nearness to London. The rapid change in the river scene between 1890 and 1897 is illustrated by the photographs.

The Thames

Below: THE VIEW FROM THE LINCOLN ARMS HOTEL 1890
23589

Punting and rowing on the Thames were very popular. These Victorian young ladies in their finery are accompanied by young men in traditional white flannels, striped blazers and straw boaters. The picnic basket in the foreground, probably from the Lincoln Arms, is well supplied for an enjoyable afternoon on the river. The rural nature of Weybridge is well shown here, with views across the river to fields and farm buildings.

WEYBRIDGE
The Thames

The Thames

The Boat Station 1903 49908

There are plenty of boats for hire, and the two people in the punt are using paddles instead of a pole — including the lady, who prefers to do her share rather than lean back on the padded seat in front. The Thames Valley Launch Company now has electric wires crossing the river to light its premises, and there is also a tall telephone mast in front of the building. The house in the distance became the lock-keeper's house in 1940 after the original one built in 1883 was damaged by enemy action.

The Thames

Seeing the potential for developing leisure activity on the river, in 1895 the Thames Valley Launch Company built a very large boathouse, called Riverside Works, next to Nicholls and Searle (see 40009, right). The company advertised itself as being designers and builders of electric, oil and steam launches and sailing boats. It had a fleet of 30 launches for hire, and it provided dressing rooms, lockers and every accommodation for customers in new premises, lit throughout by electricity. This firm catered for the wealthier river visitors; it was wound up in 1904 when electric boating became less popular. The building was bought in 1913 by Arthur A D Lang and his partner, David Garrett, to manufacture aircraft propellers. A skilled workforce was readily available from among the boatbuilders, who were skilled in bending and laminating timber, the material used for these early propellers. The building was later used by the Airscrew Company, but it was burnt down in 1942.

Downstream of the lock is The Eyot, popularly known as D'Oyly Carte Island (see 49906, page 18-19). Although Richard D'Oyly Carte could not use the house as an hotel, he would come at weekends with members of the Savoy Opera Company to stay in the house and rehearse Gilbert and Sullivan operas. This gave Weybridge residents strolling along the towpath on a Sunday evening a chance to enjoy musical treats. The only access to the island was by boat or punt from the Weybridge bank. The house remained in the ownership of Richard D'Oyly Carte until the 1920s. It was then bought by Sir George May, and subsequently sold by his widow in 1945.

With no bridge across the Thames, the ferry was very important. A ferry is known to have existed since the 15th century, when it was used to convey cattle and sheep in a flat punt across the river from Shepperton to Weybridge where the grazing was better. From 1866, the ferry became open for public use. People crossing to shop, to visit relations or to work preferred the shorter river crossing to travelling via the bridge at Walton.

Plans were drawn up to straighten the Thames in 1911 by J Crawshaw, Surveyor to Weybridge UDC, but were not passed. It was 1935 before the Desborough Cut was opened, reducing the danger of flooding and also the time taken for barges to journey from Weybridge to Kingston. Altering the river, however, destroyed the bathing places, which had been in existence since 1900. At that time the Thames Conservancy had offered to erect a bathing place 88 yards east of Gypsy Lane (downstream of D'Oyly Carte Island).

The Thames

BOATHOUSES 1897 40009

It is only seven years following picture 23589 (page 13), but in this photograph, taken from the same place, the landscape has changed. Nicholls and Searle have become Nicholls and Son, and next to them a large building belonging to the Thames Valley Launch Company Limited has been built.

The Thames

Above: THE EYOT 1903 49906

The Eyot (meaning island) is called after Richard D'Oyly Carte; he strengthened the banks of a small island in the River Thames below Shepperton Lock, and built this large house upon it in 1889. It was intended that the building would act as an annexe to the Savoy Hotel in London, which D'Oyly Carte owned; but no licence was granted, so the house came to be used as a private residence.

Right: THE FERRY 1904 51679

This shows both sides of the river. The punt crossed the Thames to a slipway to the right of Dunton's boathouse, and the fare was 1d. Thence it was a short walk to Shepperton Lock, where one could watch the progress of craft up and down the Thames to Chertsey or Walton. The beach in the foreground seems to be a result of inadequate dredging. It provided extra space for spectators when regattas took place.

Far Right: THE FERRY 1903 49907

This is a view across the Thames to the Shepperton or Middlesex side. George Dunton took over the run-down ferry and boatyard in 1893. The two ferry cottages to the right of the picture were knocked into one to provide accommodation for himself, his wife and seven children. He built up a flourishing ferry business, using a wide punt (we can see it on the far bank), and also a boat-building business whose output included racing punts and skiffs which were exported to Europe, Australia, South America and India.

The Thames

The river was dredged to provide shallow depth, and a punt was moored for diving. The superintendent was Professor W Clifford, an expert swimmer. The bathing place became very popular with residents and visitors, and children from St James's School learned to swim there every Friday evening in the summer. When the Thames Conservancy started digging the new channel in June 1933, the future of swimming in the Thames looked bleak; in January 1935 the UDC was given one month's notice of the termination of its licence for the bathing station at Weybridge. After the Channel was opened, bathing facilities moved to the point where the Channel and river diverged. These continued in use until a pool was opened in Walton-on-Thames in 1965.

Following the opening of the Desborough Cut, which made the river wider below Shepperton Lock, the Thames Conservancy gave permission for the installation of a chain ferry worked by a hand-wheel, as can be seen in W74010 (page 20-21). The chain ran along the river bed, secured to posts at either side. The ferry was built by Bates of Chertsey at a cost of £200. After the Second World War, boat-building was restricted by wood rationing, and this affected the boatbuilders on the river. The ferry across the Thames became uneconomic, and ceased in 1963. The Davy family, having bought Dunton's, continued their boat-building business until 1984; they then sold it to Lynn Lewis, who renamed it Nauticalia. The ferry restarted in 1986 using a powered craft; it is now a vital link in the Thames path, which covers 180 miles from the source near Kemble, Gloucestershire to the Thames barrier at Woolwich.

The Thames

WEYBRIDGE THE THAMES

THE RIVER THAMES C1955 W74010

The Thames

The River Thames c1955 W74008

Although still labelled Dunton's, the ferry and boat-building business now belongs to the Davy family. Sailing dinghies were becoming popular, and sailing clubs were established on both sides of the river. The number of small cruisers moored on the opposite bank indicates the increasing use of motor boats for pleasure from this time onwards.

Right: The Ferry c1960 W74054

A rowing boat has been used for this particular crossing, and a dock has been cut into the bank to make embarkation easier. Eyot House on D'Oyly Carte island was by this time divided into flats, and there were moorings for private craft on each side.

WEYBRIDGE

The Thames

The Thames

The Desborough Channel c1955 W74011

This straight piece of the river is known as the Desborough Channel, named after the Chairman of the Thames Conservancy, Lord Desborough of Taplow, who officially opened it in 1935. The Desborough Cut was 80ft wide and seven-tenths of a mile long. Salter's Steamers were plying from Kingston and Richmond to Chertsey, Windsor and Maidenhead, making good use of the clear, direct passage.

WEYBRIDGE THE THAMES

Ordnance Survey Map

Ordnance Survey Map

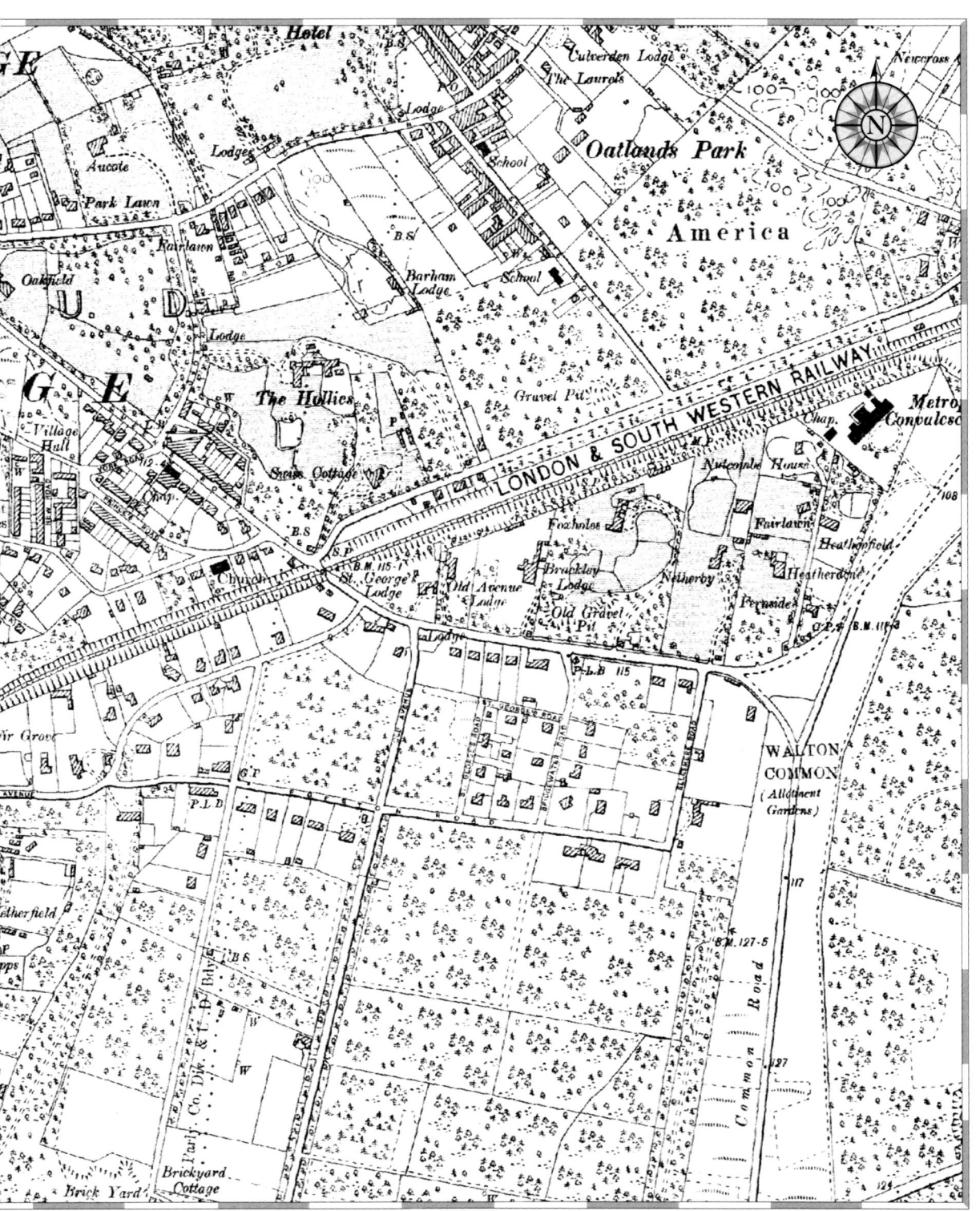

Thames to Town

Thames to Town

The Lincoln Arms Hotel 1904 51683

This hotel is at the bottom of Thames Street, facing towards the River Wey where it enters the Thames. Originally it was two early 18th-century houses, but the exact date of its becoming an inn is not known. The name refers to the Earls of Lincoln, who owned the Oatlands Park estate during the 18th century. From 1845 to 1884 the Harris family were the innkeepers; they also owned a boat-building business across the road, with a landing-stage on the River Wey.

The Lincoln Arms was one of the early public houses in Thames Street, catering for the trade associated with both rivers, the Thames and the Wey. Traditionally, the Lincoln Arms was regarded as the hostelry most suited to the wealthy patrons, whereas the Old Crown, on the opposite side of the street, was the haunt of the bargemen and poorer workers. The garden at the front of the Lincoln Arms made it a pleasant setting for relaxation after boating on the river. It still remains, but since 2000 it has been called the Minnow, thus losing its historic name, so relevant to Weybridge.

Thames Street also had two other public houses between the river and the town during the 19th century. The Portmore Arms appears on the Ordnance Survey map of Weybridge of 1869 as being at the junction of Beale's Lane and Thames Street, but the licence was transferred in 1886. The King's Arms lasted longer. Opened in the 18th century, it changed hands several times; in 1890 it was advertising itself as having 'special accommodation for pleasure parties, gardens and stabling'. Mr Gardner, who was licensee in the 1930s, acted as 'weigher-in' for Weybridge Angling Society, whose headquarters were the King's Arms. The premises were rebuilt in 1936, and renamed the Farnell Arms in 1981, but were closed and demolished in 1997.

The Portmore Pillars have suffered damage from large vehicles entering the road from Thames Street in recent years. Elmbridge Borough Council has now refurbished and cleaned them, and has erected protective bollards on adjacent pavements. Clinton House was built in 1756 by the Earl of Clinton and lived in by several notable people. It was bought in 1898 by the Sisters of the Holy Child Jesus, the Dames of St Maur, who built a convent and school in the grounds.

Thames to Town

Above: PORTMORE GATEWAY 1903 49904

These pillars are situated about halfway between the Thames and the town. They were originally part of the Portmore Park estate, which belonged to the Duke of Norfolk in the 17th century. By the 19th century the mansion was in ruins, and the estate was bought by Peter Locke King in 1861. The pillars were acquired by a Mr Ward, who bought Clinton House and land opposite in 1882. When the roads on the Portmore estate were adopted by Weybridge UDC in the 1890s, following extensive house building, Mr Ward presented the pillars to the council on condition that they were preserved as we see them in the photograph.

Right: MONUMENT GREEN c1955 W74004

The monument remains in its place, retaining the iron railings to protect it, but now with the added safety measure of concrete posts and chains. These were erected after the Second World War; many local residents objected to them on the grounds of being unsightly and unnecessary. Crown Terrace was extended by more residential building, and the view along the High Street shows the row of shops between the Ship and the Post Office. The shelter on the right was given to Weybridge in 1935 at the time of King George V's Silver Jubilee by Mr C D Strologo from Shamley Green (near Guildford). He was an Italian living in Surrey, and conscious of the English weather; so he presented about 100 of these shelters to the people of Surrey in 1935.

Thames to Town

The View from Monument Green c1965 W74097

Street lighting has been improved, and there are seats from which to enjoy the scene. A large map showing the streets of Weybridge to help visitors has now joined the oak shelter, and the bus stop outside the Ship Inn is now more prominent. The number of parked cars also reflects the increased car ownership. The roads are more clearly defined, but it is still safe enough to ride a bicycle near the middle of the road.

Monument Green 1897 40015

To the right of the monument is a drinking fountain and a tall pole (probably a drain vent) to which a gas lamp is attached. The terrace of houses behind the trees is called Crown Terrace, and was erected in 1884. Shops to the left of the Ship Inn were J W Grigg (draper), Randall (coal, coke and confectionery), Rambridge (greengrocer and beer seller), Brown and Sons (oil and colour merchants) and Tappin (greengrocer).

Thames to Town

Thames to Town

Left: THE SHIP HOTEL C1965 W74092

This full frontal view shows the name clearly written on the building itself in addition to a mural over the main entrance. The sign standing on the pavement near the bus stop carries a model ship, which has been there since at least 1931, and a more recent picture beneath it. At this time the Ship was owned by Scottish and Newcastle Breweries Ltd; extensions were added in 1971. The present owners are the Desborough Hotel Group, earlier owners celebrated 260 years of the Ship's existence in 1989. Beside the inn-sign is a time-clock used by London Transport drivers to record their journeys.

Above: THE SHIP C1960 W74050

The hotel at this time was owned by Younger and Co Ltd of Edinburgh. What had once been an important stop for horse-drawn coaches is now an important stop for London Transport buses and Green Line Coaches, as the queue indicates.

Thames to Town

Monument Green lies between Thames Street and the High Street. It was formerly known as Bull Ring Square, and has always been a focal point for this end of the village. The landmark here is the monument, which was erected in 1822 in memory of the Duchess of York; she had lived at Oatlands since her marriage to the Duke in 1791 until her death in 1820. She had no children of her own, but she supported and paid for the education of some of the local children. There were 40 of these, aged between 8 and 12, in attendance at her funeral, wearing suits of mourning provided by the Duke.

The monument itself started life in the Seven Dials region of London in 1694, following the Great Fire. It was removed during a fruitless search for treasure believed to be buried underneath it, and it was bought by the architect James Payne in 1774. The rest of the story is linked with the Ship Inn.

The most interesting building at this end of the High Street is the Ship Inn; the earliest reference to it occurs in 1729. Its name may be related to the number of senior naval officers living locally, and the Ship was used for recruiting volunteers during the Napoleonic wars. It was a coach stop in horse-drawn days, providing accommodation and refreshment. A regular service arrived from Addlestone and departed for London at 8.15am every day except Sunday. The return trip from Fleet Street left at 3.30pm, arriving at the Ship at 7.15pm. The stage coach survived until at least 1867, despite the coming of the railway.

Mr Todd, the landlord of the Ship in 1820, had ambitious ideas for commemorating the life of the late Duchess of York and made a collection in the village for this. Not enough money was raised to fulfil his dreams, so he bought the column and capstone originating from Seven Dials; by then, they were owned by a stonemason living and working near the Ship. The capstone was removed and replaced by a pinnacle incorporating a ducal coronet.

From the Ship Hotel the High Street leads into the main shopping area. It was several years before this road took on a modern aspect. The left-hand side of the High Street was occupied by small houses and cottages — Sussex Villas, Nutfield Cottages and Avenue Villas. Numbers 3 and 4 Avenue Villas housed the National Telephone Company between 1902 and 1912. Puttock's carriage works, which had started in part of the grounds of Orchard House in about 1850, remained until 1915. The cottages were demolished to make way for

a parade of shops, including Woolworth's, in 1939. The outbreak of war prevented these opening as planned, and the Woolworth's shop was used by employees from the firm's London headquarters who had been evacuated to the country for safety.

The buildings adjacent to the Ship itself were small shops, ending in Webb's Farm on the corner of Elmgrove Road. This had been associated with the Portmore Estate, but was incongruous in a developing townscape. In 1912 a new Post Office was built on the site; the building still stands today, but it is now an estate agency, although the rear buildings are still used as a sorting office.

Thames to Town

High Street 1906 55657

The major building on the left is Holstein Hall, newly built in 1904/5 in the grounds of Holstein House (later demolished) by a local caterer, J Wiltshire, to act as a venue for local entertainments and gatherings. The hall opened in January 1905 with a performance of Mendelssohn's 'Elijah' given by Weybridge Choral Society. With a sprung floor and a platform, it continued to be used for various local activities, including two meetings dealing with women's right to vote. Christabel Pankhurst spoke in favour of women's suffrage in 1910. The following year an anti-suffrage meeting was held by the Weybridge and District Branch of the National League for Opposing Woman Suffrage, with various local ladies, including Mrs Locke King, taking part. The parade of shops beyond Holstein Hall was built in 1904, and consisted of five shops with living accommodation above. In 1906 these were a china and glass shop (Holstein Stores), E Wade's footwear, Hicks' dairy, Chitty and Hodges (butchers) and W Levermore (cycle manufacturer).

Thames to Town

Thames to Town

High Street c1955 W74032 (with details)

Holstein Hall still exists, but it has become a motor showroom and garage. Its use as a meeting room and concert hall declined after 1913, and it was auctioned; it was not sold until 1917, when Vickers bought it as an extra aeroplane workshop. After the First World War the hall remained empty until 1923, when Samuel Wood bought it to extend his garage business. It opened as a showroom in 1924. A petrol pump can be seen on the pavement outside, and there are advertisements for Vauxhall, Rover and Buick cars.

Thames to Town

Thames to Town

High Street c1965 W74101

Holstein Hall has now been replaced by a Fine Fare supermarket and a Singer Sewing machine shop. The parade built in 1904 still stands, containing a bakery, a shoe shop and Kett's electrical store. On the right is Beethams, outfitters, whose shop has been there since 1898. Further shops include Addlestone Co-operative Society, Burtons, Robert Dyas, Boots the chemists, Woolworth's and Pedley and White (hardware).

The Town Centre

Baker Street 1903 49902

The Town Centre

Above: THE SCHOOLS 1906 55649

The schools date back to 1813, when a National School took over premises formerly occupied by Miss Hopton's charity school and provided elementary education for boys and girls. It was closely linked with the parish church.

As the village population increased during the 19th century, the buildings were added to in 1850, 1866 and 1894, providing separate accommodation for boys, girls and infants. By 1906 the schools were also providing secondary education; they were known as Weybridge Church of England Schools.

Baker Street joins the main road through Weybridge where High Street becomes Church Street. It was known as Loampit Lane, Shelton Lane and Back Street before it acquired its present name.

The London and County Bank was built in 1897, following the success of earlier sub-branches in various shops in the High Street. The bank purchased the freehold of No 1 High Street from Mr John Sother for £1,230 in 1889 and employed W Campbell Jones to design the building; it was constructed by W H Gaze and Sons at a cost of £3,985. The bank is now the NatWest.

Opposite the London and County Bank was Aberdeen House, home to W Dale and Sons, butchers (see 49902, left). In 1908 the right-hand part of the building (a house) was sold to Weybridge UDC to become the Council Offices and Weybridge Museum. The building was demolished in 1967 after the Council Offices moved to a new Town Hall in Walton-on-Thames and the museum and library

The Town Centre

moved to new premises further along Church Street. The building was replaced by shops and Lloyds Bank.

Halfway up Baker Street on the right were the schools (see 55649, page 41), and opposite them was Springfield Cottage. In 1953 the school was reorganised, and a mixed secondary school used the former boys' school building. In 1966 the secondary school moved to purpose-built premises in Brooklands Lane and took the name Heathside Secondary School. The old buildings remained as a middle school until this in turn moved to new premises in Grotto Road in 1981. The original school buildings were then demolished; sheltered accommodation, called Bridge Court, was built on most of the site. Two original school cottages remain.

Baker Street has always been an area for small shops, often specialising in unusual products as well as the more mundane. In 1904 these included a watchmaker, a milliner, and a picture-frame maker, in addition to a butcher, builder, saddler, corn merchant and florist, fishmonger and baker. A similar mixture of shops can be seen in the 1965 photo (W74098, page 44) where we have insurance brokers, ladies' boutiques, knitwear, delicatessen, estate agents and Roberts Dyas, ironmongers. In the distance, in Church Street, is a supermarket; it was built following the demolition in 1962 of the Newcastle Arms, a public house dating from the late 18th century.

A side road from Baker Street leads to Churchfields, the site of a recreation ground and car park. The distinctive building next to the recreation ground is the Technical Institute. The bowling green seen in photograph W74034, page 45, was laid out in the seven-acre recreation ground which had been given to Weybridge in 1908 by Mr J Lyle, the sugar refiner, who lived at Finnart House. The terms of the gift were to provide an area for young people and the elderly to relax; the proposal to include a bowling green was held to conflict with these terms, and met with some local opposition at the time.

The recreation ground was known as Churchfields because of its proximity to the parish church; it was laid out with seats, grass and flower beds. An oak tree was planted in the grounds by Mr Lyle in honour of the coronation of George V in 1911, together with a purple beech tree planted by John Durant, who was thought to be the oldest inhabitant of Weybridge at the time.

Baker Street 1904 51688

On becoming Weybridge UDC in 1895, the Council needed to find premises for offices; they were offered the use of the two houses on the left, Haisboro and Benvenuta. It is possible that only one of the houses was in use at this time — the other is advertising the services of the previous occupant, a ladies' tailor and dressmaker. In 1903 the Council arranged to widen Baker Street, which at its narrowest point was only 21ft wide. The work on this is probably the reason for the wheelbarrow, spade and heap of soil we can see, as well as the partially-built fence in front of the houses. Beyond the houses is Shanks, motor engineers and J M Ansell, coal merchant.

The Town Centre

The Town Centre

Above: BAKER STREET c1965 W74098

The buildings remain much as they were earlier; only the shop fronts have changed. Robert Dyas's long narrow shop had frontages on both High Street and Baker Street.

Right: THE TECHNICAL INSTITUTE c1955 W74033

There was a Technical Institute in Elmgrove Road in 1903, but the local Council and also the County Council agreed to pay for a new building to be erected next to the open land known as Churchfields. The new Technical Institute was opened in November 1912. It provided technical training for children from local elementary schools, including woodwork for boys and cooking, laundry and housekeeping for girls. With its distinctive bell turret the building has remained a landmark in the centre of Weybridge.

The Town Centre

The Church 1904 51692

The Rector at the time this picture was taken was the Rev Spencer Buller (1903-1924). The view is across the Rectory garden to the north side of the church.

The Bowling Green and Churchfields Pleasure Gardens c1955 W74034

THE TOWN CENTRE

Above: THE PARISH CHURCH c1955 W74041

This view of the parish church is from the north-west. The building on the right is the Midland Bank; between it and the churchyard is a narrow passage, now called Church Lane, leading to the south door of the church. The churchyard was full by the 1870s, so additional cemetery space was bought and chapels erected in Brooklands Lane in 1876. There are several interesting monuments in the churchyard; some of them remain from the earlier church, when they would have been inside the building. Among these is the vault, surrounded by railings, containing the remains of the Duchess of York, buried in 1820.

Below: THE PARISH CHURCH c1955 W74035

This view of the parish church is taken from the east, across allotments which have since become a necessary car park in the centre of the town. The church now has a Parish Centre where the pine tree is growing, providing well-equipped halls and rooms for parish and community use.

The Town Centre

Church Street was the centre of village life in the 18th century with the church, rectory and large houses of the gentry. When the village began to grow in the 19th century, the new Rector, William Giffard, appointed in 1846, saw the need for a larger parish church; he persuaded the wealthier residents to subscribe towards this, despite some opposition from the older villagers. The parish church of St James was built in 1848 to accommodate the growing population of Weybridge. The smaller, earlier church of St Nicholas occupied a site nearer Church Street; it was demolished after the new church was opened. The architect was John Loughborough Pearson, who later went on to build Truro cathedral. The original St James's Church was added to several times - the spire was completed in 1856, a peal of bells was given in 1874, and the chancel was lengthened in 1888. An annual celebration of St James's Day, 25 July, began in 1884 and still continues.

The wall of the churchyard can be seen again in photograph 49903. Behind the trees lies the Rectory, today tastefully refurbished and used as offices. The brick wall on the opposite side of the street conceals Vigo House, built by Admiral Hopson in the 18th century and named after a naval victory of 1802 in which he participated.

The cottage hospital in Balfour Road, which served the town until Weybridge hospital was built in Church Street in 1928, became the Locke King Clinic in recognition of the generosity of Hugh Locke

CHURCH STREET 1903 49903

Clay's grocery stores form the first shop in a row built in 1899 by E H Thompson, and called Queen's Parade. Bennett's, next door, was a confectioners; it was used as a forces canteen during the First World War. J W Barron (drapers), Standages (newsagent and stationers), London's Provincial Meat Co and Stowells (wine merchant) completed the parade. The bath chair in the picture foreground is standing outside Ye Olde Curiosity Shoppe, which was acquired by the Gem family in 1886. It was a marvellous treasure house of all sorts of objects, including antiques, furniture and joinery, all displayed in a haphazard manner both inside the shop and outside on the pavement. Bicycles and bath chairs were also available for hire.

The Town Centre

King. It continued to be a valuable addition to the town's medical facilities until the opening of a new and larger hospital; this included all primary care departments, and was built on the Church Street site in 1999. The 1928 hospital was then demolished, and the former Locke King Clinic was converted into offices. Shops beyond the hospital include Buckling's bakery, Savory & Moore (chemists), Freeman, Hardy & Willis (footwear), Howard's Fish shop and a new supermarket.

The more modern views of Church Street show the same alignment of buildings, but the lime trees have gone (despite a petition against this signed by 137 residents in 1934), and there is much more activity and evidence of transport. Bicycles, motor-cars and buses have arrived, although the sight of a double-decker bus in Weybridge is unusual; this follows a request in 1924 that only single-decker buses should pass through the town because of the lighting fittings.

CHURCH STREET c1965 W74103

The brick gateways guard the entrance to Weybridge Hospital, built on the site of Vigo House and opened in 1928.

The Town Centre

Church Street c1955 W74037

At this time, the County Cinema is located in the former Clay's stores. The building was used during the First World War by Gordon Watney Engineering Co, but then remained empty until 1920 when it was converted into a cinema. Improvements to seating and accommodation were made in 1927, when it became the King George's Cinema, showing the first talkie films. Ten years later, the name was changed to the County Cinema. Thus it remained, until the building was converted by the council into a public hall in 1956; it is still a public hall today.

Towards the Heath

The Quadrant 1904 51686

TOWARDS THE HEATH

Church Street bends to follow the line of the churchyard and turns towards the Heath and the railway station to the South. Although the London and Southampton Railway followed a line across Weybridge Heath and divided the village from St George's Hill, the company directors were reluctant to provide a station at Weybridge, since they did not expect it to be much used. They agreed to build a simple station at the bottom of an incline as a temporary measure; only later, in 1857, did they build a more permanent structure next to the road bridge over the tracks, with 60 steps down to the platform.

Entering Weybridge from the south and the station, one would have seen the row of buildings straight ahead (51686). Built in the late 1880s and 1890s, the pleasing curve of shops with accommodation above consisted of nine properties. George Gates, whose shop-blind is most clearly seen, was a fishmonger at No 5. To the right at No 4 was a fruiterer, Mr White; there was a hairdresser and Post Office at No 3, the Court Creamery at No 2 and Thomas Dix, butcher, at No 1. The large house behind the brick wall on the right was called The Limes; it was the lodging place of the novelist George Meredith after his marriage in 1849.

The attractive area known as the Quadrant is situated where Church Street joins the road leading to the station, on the site of the former entrance to Portmore Park. This had been one of the large estates in Weybridge, covering an area between Thames Street and the River Wey; the mansion deteriorated during the early 19th century, and it was demolished in 1826. The estate was bought by local landowner Peter Locke King in 1861 for £8,000. Later his son, Hugh Fortesque Locke King, sold off the estate in separate parcels of land to be developed as housing from 1881 onwards.

The Quadrant area was a favourite spot for promenading, chatting, shopping and relaxing during the 1900s. Church Street was at that time the main road out of Weybridge to the west, leading to the bridge across the Wey. With grass areas, seats and the old hostelry, the Queen's Head, close by, it was a popular part of the town. The lime trees were a particular feature of this area.

By 1955 the shops of the Quadrant itself have changed (next page), but the buildings retain their Victorian charm. The Southern Electric sign points along Heath Road towards the railway station. The railway, opened in 1838, was, of course, initially steam operated; the change to electric traction for local services came in 1937.

Towards the Heath

Above: THE QUADRANT AND LIMES PARADE c1955 W74039

The most obvious change from 51686 (page 50-51) is the replacement of The Limes, which was demolished in 1908/9, by a parade of shops known as Limes Parade, built in 1910. Some of the lime trees have also gone; but now seats have been provided so that townsfolk can enjoy the area, and there are innovations in the form of a telephone kiosk and a pillar box. Burden and Parker, the Murphy television and radio dealers on the right, also indicates the modern means of entertainment and communication; Humphris, near right, was a jewellers.

Above Right: CHURCH STREET c1955 W74040

Motor-cars have replaced the horse-drawn carriages, and the Quadrant Motors sign on the left indicates the entrance to a yard behind the shops where maintenance and repairs were carried out. There is a bus stop near the seated man; this was for the regular service from Kingston, a major shopping area, through the centre of Weybridge and onwards to the station. In the distance can be seen Portmore House, an 18th-century listed building, originally on the Portmore Park estate. The clock, centre left, was erected in 1932 by Savory's the clothiers at No 1 The Quadrant — it was also used to mark the bus stop.

Below Right: CHURCH STREET c1955 W74038

This photograph was taken at the same time as the others of the Quadrant area, as the elderly man sitting on the seat shows. Several long-standing traders who were a feature of Weybridge had their premises here. H F Luxford's removal firm started in the 1920s, taking over a business started by John Stainton of Oatlands, and is still a family business. The building with the canopy was a butcher's shop belonging to Thomas Dix, a business which started in Weybridge in 1836 when Robert Dix rented several acres of land to graze cattle. The alley between Luxfords and the shop with the blind led to an abattoir behind Dix's shop. Above the shops towers the spire of St James's Parish Church, completed in 1856, a prominent landmark to visitors approaching Weybridge from the west.

Towards the Heath

Towards the Heath

On the River Wey 1904 51677

This is typical of the rural river scenes at Weybridge at the turn of the century, before the First World War. Large houses had access to the river, and often had their own picturesque boathouses. The one in this picture is particularly attractive with its thatched roofs and boat moored underneath.

A Boat Station on the Wey 1897 40013

This view illustrates the peaceful and rural attractiveness of the Wey. Nicholls's boathouse is an elaborate structure, with a balcony above the landing stage; its doors are open, and the boats in serried ranks await the day's customers.

Towards the Heath

The Old Bridge c1955 W74046

The Victorian iron bridge on the right crosses the River Wey. The Wey Navigation disappears on the extreme right of the picture into Town Lock. The quay opposite was owned by Eastwoods, builders' merchants, from at least 1899, with the wharf being used to unload materials up to the 1960s. Boats for hire in the foreground of the picture were popular for rowing under the bridge and up the winding River Wey, often reaching the very high railway bridge and the beginning of the aircraft works.

The last regular steam service (to Bournemouth) passed through Weybridge in July 1967.

The River Wey and the Victorian bridge were only a short step from the Quadrant. It is here that the 17th-century river improvement scheme mentioned earlier becomes evident as the course of the river separates from that of the navigation. The river flows from under the bridge, and was popular for rowing and punting. Large houses were built with access to the river — see 51677, above left.

Wooden bridges crossing the Wey were known from at least 1571, when a bridge 240ft long and 5ft 3inches wide was the Queen's responsibility to maintain, since she was the owner of the adjoining manors. This bridge was reconstructed in 1808 with 13 wooden arches. A stronger and more durable bridge was needed by the mid 19th century because of the increases in population and traffic; W74046, above, shows the bridge, which was built in 1865. The 'official' opening of the bridge on 31 July 1865 was somewhat unusual: a costermonger, Henry Roake from Chertsey, is reported to have stood up on his donkey cart and pronounced the bridge 'open to the public for ever and a day'.

By the 1930s, further increases in traffic showed the need for a wider and stronger bridge to cope with heavy motorised transport. A new route was designed to extend Balfour Road from its junction with Church Street to a new bridge about 200yds north of the old bridge. Although started in 1939, this was not finished until after

Towards the Heath

the Second World War. The wider road and bridge have by-passed the old bridge, leaving it more peaceful and a continuing reminder of leisurely Victorian times.

Having passed through the Town Lock, cruising boats can proceed upstream to Guildford or even to Godalming, a journey of 19 miles with 14 locks. Weybridge is soon left behind.

Moving towards the railway station along Heath Road, the road starts to go uphill; on the right is an expanse of common. The common was part of the Poor's Land, granted under the Enclosure Act of 1800. Cottages built facing the common had names like Railway Terrace (although they were not very close to the station), Walnut Cottage, Pine Cottages and Holly Cottages. The large building in picture 40017 (page 58-59) is the Roman Catholic church of St Charles Borromeo. James Taylor had built his own chapel in 1835 so that his family could worship according to the rites of the Roman Catholic Church. Under the Roman Catholic Emancipation Act of 1829 this was allowed, provided that such buildings had no bells or steeple. This early chapel was therefore modelled on the Chapel Royal of St Louis at Dreux in Normandy. The building was registered as a place of worship in 1841; it was honoured by the presence of Louis Phillipe, ex-King of the French, and his family after 1848. From 1850, several members of the French royal family were interred in the crypt. As the Roman Catholic community in Weybridge increased, larger premises were needed, so the church we see in the picture was built, hiding the earlier chapel from view.

Between the church and the village was the Mitre Inn, built around 1860 and demolished 2004. The emblem of the inn was the arms of Chertsey Abbey, with the keys of St Peter and the sword of St Paul on the background of a mitred abbot. Chertsey Abbey was destroyed at the Dissolution of the Monasteries in 1537/8, but the Mitre Inn continued the religious associations of the area.

Towards the Heath

The Wey Navigation c1955 W74042

The open lock is the Town Lock on the Wey Navigation. The boat which has just come through is on its way upstream towards New Haw, and perhaps eventually Guildford. Watching boats is always an absorbing pastime, as the family on the right shows.

Towards the Heath

On the Common 1897 40017

This area of common lies between the village and the railway station. The church, centre left, is the Roman Catholic church of St Charles Borromeo, built in 1881 onto the older private chapel owned by the Taylor family.

Towards the Heath

TOWARDS THE HEATH

Above: ST CHARLES'S CHURCH, THE INTERIOR 1904 51696

This is the interior of the 1881 addition to St Charles Borromeo church; the pictures on the walls show the stations of the cross. No attempt was made to match the original chapel — the addition followed the Gothic Revival style. The stained glass windows depict, among many others, the patron saints of each member of the Taylor family.

Right: HEATH ROAD c1960 W74058

We are looking downhill from the direction of the railway station towards the town centre. The church of St Charles Borromeo is on the right; behind the brick wall is Waverley Cottage, formerly the presbytery for the Catholic priests and originally the family home of the Taylors. Today the 1881 building is used by the Korean Presbyterian church; the Roman Catholic congregation now has a modern church, Christ the Prince of Peace, dedicated in 1989, together with presbytery, hall and school, in Portmore Park Road.

Towards the Heath

County Map

A Section of a County Map of Surrey showing Weybridge and surrounding areas c1850

County Map

Upper Weybridge

The Cricket Common 1903 49905

The trees and seats on the Common were given to the people of Weybridge in 1887 by Henry Yool, local resident and benefactor, in celebration of Queen Victoria's Golden Jubilee. The delivery cart and the child with the large basket are probably associated with J Wiltshire's bakery, which opened in 1881 facing the Common.

Upper Weybridge

The Common appears on maps as The Green as late as 1934/5, but because cricket had been played there on and off since the 1850s, it was popularly referred to as the Cricket Common. The landlord of the Stag and Hounds, situated near the corner of the Common, is credited with encouraging cricket from about 1850, and there was a club in existence in 1857. An account of a cricket match played in 1864 between Weybridge and the Donkey Artillery was described in the Surrey Comet: 'A match is advertised between 12 Gentlemen of Weybridge and 12 Players of Weybridge to take place on Weybridge Common on Tuesday 30 May 1882, wickets to be pitched punctually at 11 o'clock'.

The cricket club was a long time in acquiring a pavilion, despite requests to the Council for such an amenity in the 1940s. The problem was partly due to difficulty in establishing the exact ownership of the Common, and it was not until 1953 that the pavilion was built. The Common attracted further development around it, encouraged by important roads on two sides; these were Queen's Road, the main route to Hersham, Esher and Kingston, and the road to the station. Station Road was so called until the residents of the road petitioned the Council in 1921 to change the name to Hanger Hill, which they felt created a better image.

Upper Weybridge

Right and Below: THE CRICKET COMMON c1955 W74024

This view, taken from the pavilion, shows supporters relaxing in deck chairs, and a batsman with pads awaiting his turn. On the far side of the common, the Stag and Hounds public house can be glimpsed between the trees and nearby York House cafe, which occupies the former Wiltshire's bakery.

Upper Weybridge

Left and Below: THE COMMON c1955
W74020

The railings, seats and trees are the same as 49905, page 64-65, except that the last have grown considerably. The Cricket Club now has a pavilion, and the ground is professionally looked after; matches are played regularly in the summer. Behind the pavilion are the trees of Manby Lodge, a large house fronting Queen's Road. The large houses to the right are Leavesden and St Catherine's (formerly St Michael's House).

Upper Weybridge

Upper Weybridge

The View from Prince's House c1960 W74063

This shows more clearly the line of shops facing the Cricket Common across Hanger Hill. The war memorial can be seen on the right, and Temple Market behind it. This was built in the 1930s, and was so called because of its somewhat classical appearance. Temple Market shops included Kinghams (grocers), Dorothy (florist) and Mrs Grundy's Tea-rooms.

Upper Weybridge

Upper Weybridge

Above: PRINCE'S HOUSE c1960 W74065

Situated at the junction of Prince's Road and Hanger Hill, this was formerly called The Birches. By the 1960s it was divided into flats and bedsits. It has subsequently been demolished and replaced by blocks of flats called Prince's Court. The grassy area in the foreground is the present-day location of the Yool memorial.

Left: THE MEMORIAL c1955 W74023

The war memorial, placed on a triangle between Hanger Hill and Queen's Road, was unveiled in 1923, after much discussion and debate. The soldier surmounting the memorial has his back to the cricket match — which still seems popular, as we can see from the number of bicycles and parked cars.

Upper Weybridge

Upper Weybridge

The Yool Memorial 1906 55650

This fountain stood at the top of Monument Hill. It was erected in 1896 in memory of Henry Yool, a local benefactor and Vice-Chairman of the newly-formed Surrey County Council from 1889-92. The attractive building behind the memorial is Albany Cottage.

On the far side of the Cricket Common stands the war memorial. It is of Portland stone, standing 16ft high and surmounted by a statue of a soldier facing towards the top of Monument Hill. General A F Gatlif unveiled the memorial in March 1923. There were 135 names on it at that time. Present at the unveiling ceremony were about 140 ex-servicemen, the Fire Brigade, a detachment from the 6th East Surrey Regiment, and local Guides and Scouts. Subsequently, names of local servicemen killed in the Second World War and the Korean War have been added.

Not far from the war memorial stood the Yool fountain. Henry Yool lived at Oakfield, near the site of his memorial, for most of his time in Weybridge, but at the time of his death in December 1894 he had recently had a house called Field Place built to the south of the railway station. He had contributed to the life of the village in many ways, including allowing fetes and similar functions to be held in the grounds of Oakfield; he was elected as the first councillor for Weybridge when Surrey County Council was established after the 1888 Local Government Act.

The Grotto Inn 1906 55648

The Grotto Inn began its life as an alehouse early in the 19th century. It was connected with several brewers from 1877, including Hodgsons Kingston Brewery Ltd, as we see in the photograph. In about 1900 the frontage was altered, with gables, half-timbering and leaded lights all being added to make it appear more fashionable. It also began advertising teas and refreshments, presumably to widen its trade.

Upper Weybridge

Oatlands Park Hotel
1906 55655

The hotel was formerly Oatlands House; it was sold to the South Western Hotel Company following the break-up of the Oatlands estate after 1846. The hotel has always been a popular venue for the wealthy, with its extensive grounds and superior accommodation. The tree to the left of the hotel was advertised in a series of publicity postcards in the early 1900s as 'The first Cedar of Lebanon in England, planted by Prince Henry of Oatlands'. This is unlikely, since Prince Henry was born in 1640, 3rd son of King Charles I and Queen Henrietta Maria, at Oatlands Palace, which was about half a mile away from Oatlands House; it was demolished in 1650.

The people of Weybridge held a meeting in June 1895 to decide on a suitable memorial for Mr Yool, and the first suggestion was to build a technical institute to be named after him. This idea proved impractical, so a fountain was agreed upon. The Metropolitan Drinking Fountain and Cattle Trough Association was approached to provide a suitable monument. This was installed at a cost of £195; it bore the inscription, 'Erected by the Parishioners in memory of Henry Yool of Field Place, Weybridge, 1896'. The fountain remained in its original position until March 1971, by which time it was no longer providing drinking water; it was moved to a small island at the junction of Hanger Hill and Prince's Road. Field Place remained in the Yool family until Mrs Yool died in 1930. A new estate of large houses was begun on the site in 1932, but it was not completed until after the Second World War.

Also near the top of Monument Hill at its junction with Baker Street is the Grotto Inn. The name refers to the 18th-century grotto built in the grounds of Oatlands House by the Earl of Lincoln. It was elaborate and extensive, containing several rooms and a large bath dominated by a statue of Venus de Medici. The grotto was demolished in 1948 following neglect and vandalism, but the statue remains in Elmbridge Museum.

UPPER WEYBRIDGE

OATLANDS DRIVE C1955 W74022

The Yool memorial on the right is here being used to support a signpost and lamp standard; its purpose as a drinking fountain seems to have been overtaken by more modern needs. The 19th-century houses on the left have become commercial premises and shops, among them The Cake Bowl (tea-room), Evans (tobacconist and confectioner), and Collyer (hairdressers and chiropodist). Griffin's Garage had showrooms and workshops on the left and a petrol station opposite, marked by the Shell and BP signs.

Oatlands House was built in the 18th century by the 7th Earl of Lincoln, who also had the grounds landscaped and the famous grotto built. The estate was sold to Frederick, Duke of York, in 1788. He married Princess Frederica of Prussia in 1791, and she remained at Oatlands for the rest of her life. The house was damaged by fire in 1794, and parts were rebuilt and altered. After the death of the Duchess of York, the Duke sold the estate in 1824. The purchaser, Edward Hughes Ball Hughes, subsequently got into financial difficulties, and the estate was divided into 64 lots which were offered for sale at auction in 1846. The area had by this time become attractive for residential development on account of the easy rail access to London. The house itself became the Oatlands Park Hotel in 1856. It has remained an hotel ever since, attracting well-known visitors and special events such as the Ladies' Motor Meet held in 1903. It was also used as a military hospital in the First World War, an outpost of the New Zealand military hospital at Mount Felix in Walton-on-Thames.

The present-day main road leading from Weybridge to Walton-Thames is Oatlands Drive, passing through what had once been the Oatlands estate. The older public road linking Weybridge to Walton,

Upper Weybridge

Upper Weybridge

Oatlands Drive c1955
W74022

Upper Weybridge

Queen's Road 1906
55654

The parade of shops catered for the needs of the large houses in this upper part of Weybridge. These included A Burningham, wine merchant, W Sharp, baker (the canopy furthest from the camera), Jarvis and Mackie, corn merchants, J Williams, tailor (on these premises since 1876), Emma Hull, draper and outfitter from the same date, J Kennett, chemist, and a fish shop, owned in 1906 by George Gates, later by Mowatts. Displaying goods outside shops on the pavement was a feature of the times, as were the horse-drawn delivery carts taking advantage of the improved road surface.

Hersham and Esher was Queen's Road — the name was adopted at the time of Queen Victoria's Diamond Jubilee in 1897. Formerly it had been called The Grange. It leads from the Cricket Common and the top of Monument Hill eastwards towards Hersham and Esher; it was used by Queen Victoria when she travelled from Windsor to Claremont, the home of her son and daughter-in-law, the Duke and Duchess of Albany.

Queen's Road was surfaced in 1905 by Weybridge UDC, hence its level appearance in the photographs. The Congregational Church was built in 1864/5 at the junction of Queen's Road with York Road. All the

Upper Weybridge

Below: QUEEN'S ROAD 1906 55651

This entrance to a large property, complete with lodge and gates, was typical of the residential development along Queen's Road from the 1850s onwards. This particular lodge stood at the entrance to Oatlands Avenue from Queen's Road, an area known as 'America' on 19th-century maps because of its supposed likeness to the wooded areas of North America.

properties on the same side of the road were large houses built from the 1880s onwards; the one next to the church was Rackenford Lodge.

Large houses built along Queen's Road beyond Haines Bridge (named after the bailiff of the Oatlands estate at the time of its sale in 1846) included St George's Lodge, Old Avenue Lodge, Brackley, Foxholes and Holmwood (later Netherby). One by one all of these were sold, demolished and the sites re-developed after the Second World War. The resulting estates, interspersed with smaller houses, varied from architect-designed landscaped areas to blocks of flats or Council-owned special accommodation for the elderly in bungalows surrounding a grassed area.

The 1955 views overleaf show that the nature and atmosphere of Queen's Road has been retained by the continuing use of small shops and lack of re-development. The Odeon cinema (W74025, page 80-81, centre) was built in 1934, and seated over 900 people. It remained a cinema until 1960; it was then converted into a Roman Catholic church, dedicated to St Martin de Porres. Having served its purpose until a new complex of Roman Catholic buildings was opened in 1989, the building was subsequently demolished, and a block of offices was added to the existing terrace of shops with flats above, known as Oakfield Court.

Upper Weybridge

Queen's Road c1955 W74025

Motor-cars are now part of the scenery, and so are bicycles. The line of shops has not changed since 1906, but the occupiers have. The wine merchant, baker and corn & feed merchant remain, but the Westminster Bank has arrived (detail below). Barwicks the stationers also runs the Temple Library, where books may be borrowed at a charge of 2d per week.

Upper Weybridge

Upper Weybridge

Upper Weybridge

Queen's Road c1955 W74026

This view complements photograph W74025, page 80-81; it was taken at the same time, but looks along the line of shops in the opposite direction. The Duke of York public house (detail, below) was originally opened in the 1860s, but was replaced in the 1920s by the present building, which is just visible. The landlord at this time was E G Western of the Western Brothers, formerly popular radio entertainers. Beyond the Duke of York is Brocklesby (greengrocer), Walters (butchers), Sheards (drapers), Winser (optician) and United Dairies.

Upper Weybridge

Upper Weybridge

The dominant building opposite the shops in Queen's Road was the Congregational church, which was built in 1864/65. It was designed to hold 350 people, and was equipped with a Willis pipe organ, which was played by its builder at the opening service. Behind the church was a building used as a lecture hall, Sunday School and, from 1871, the Weybridge British School. A gallery was added to the church in 1886 because of the need for more pews. In 1972 the Congregational Church in England and Wales joined with the Presbyterian Church of England to form the United Reformed Church, which it remains; this church is the only place of worship in this upper part of Weybridge.

The Congregational Church c1955 W74030

The Congregational Church was opened for worship in 1865, largely owing to the endeavour and generosity of Benjamin Scott, Chamberlain of the City of London, who had been living in Heath House, Station Road, since 1854. The architect was John Tarring, who was responsible for several non-conformist chapels in south-east England. The church was built at a cost of £2,100, including all fees.

Names of Subscribers

The following people have kindly supported this book by purchasing limited edition copies prior to publication.

Mr and Mrs R F Alder

For Mum and Dad from Anna

Deidre E Austin-Jolly, Weybridge

The Beadle Family, Weybridge

In memory of R W Berry

Happy 60th Birthday Dad, Love from Beryl

Jeff, Ellen and Emma Bott, Weybridge

Mr N S and Mrs M Chadwick, Weybridge

Terry and Carol Charlton - fond memories

Peter Cork, Weybridge

The Couch Family, Weybridge

In Memory of Albert P Cross

Mr J T and Mrs W A Davies, Weybridge

Mr and Mrs A E Eager, Weybridge

Mr and Mrs G B Gibbs, 60 wonderful years

In memory of Hedley Hambly, Weybridge from his family

The Hibberd Family, Egham

Carol Rose Hutchings of Walton and Weybridge

Mr R G and Mrs M A Jacobs, Weybridge

Mrs P A Kelly, Weybridge

Mr and Mrs P J Lucas, Weybridge

In memory of Hugh Matthews

Paul, Sara, Cheyenne and Nathan McCarthy

The Mills and Rodd Families

Mr and Mrs M Murdoch, Weybridge

Mr D Nash, Weybridge

Mr Peter G Pritchard, Mrs Jean Pritchard

Vanessa Pritchard, née Kirk Weybridge

Miss L S Pye, Weybridge

Mr Peter Rawcliffe

The Sertin Family, Weybridge

David A Smith, Weybridge

John Stather - Oatlands

Michael and Becky Stather - Weybridge

Catherine Steele, Weybridge

David, Heather and Andrew Tucker

Mr G W and Mrs K Tuck

To many happy years spent in Weybridge

The Wingate Family

Mr and Mrs D F Winstanley, Weybridge

Mr and Mrs J M Winter

Jack Worsley

Mr and Mrs P R Wright

Tony Wyeman - Happy Birthday

Index

THE THAMES

Boathouses	16-17
The Boat Station	14-15
The Church and the River	10-11
The Desborough Channel	24-25
The Eyot	18-19
The Ferry	18-19, 22-23
The River Thames	12-13, 20-21, 22

THAMES TO TOWN

High Street	34-35, 36-37, 38-39
Monument Green	30, 31
Portmore Gateway	30
The Lincoln Arms Hotel	28-29
The Ship Hotel	32-33

THE TOWN CENTRE

Baker Street	40-41, 42-43, 44
The Bowling Green	45
The Church	45, 46
Church Street	47, 48-49
The Schools	41
The Technical Institute	44

TOWARDS THE HEATH

Church Street	53
The Common	58-59
Heath Road	60-61
The Old Bridge	55
The Quadrant	50-51, 52
The River Wey	54, 56-57
St Charles's Church	60

UPPER WEYBRIDGE

The Congregational Church	84-85
The Cricket Common	64-65, 66-67, 68-69
The Grotto Inn	73
Oatlands Drive	75, 76-77
Oatlands Park Hotel	74-75
Prince's House	71
Queen's Road	78-79, 80-81, 82-83
The War Memorial	70-71
The Yool Memorial	72-73

FRITH PRODUCTS & SERVICES

Francis Frith would doubtless be pleased to know that the pioneering publishing venture he started in 1860 still continues today. Over a hundred and forty years later, The Francis Frith Collection continues in the same innovative tradition and is now one of the foremost publishers of vintage photographs in the world. Some of the current activities include:

INTERIOR DECORATION
Today Frith's photographs can be seen framed and as giant wall murals in thousands of pubs, restaurants, hotels, banks, retail stores and other public buildings throughout the country. In every case they enhance the unique local atmosphere of the places they depict and provide reminders of gentler days in an increasingly busy and frenetic world.

PRODUCT PROMOTIONS
Frith products are used by many major companies to promote the sales of their own products or to reinforce their own history and heritage. Frith promotions have been used by Hovis bread, Courage beers, Scots Porage Oats, Colman's mustard, Cadbury's foods, Mellow Birds coffee, Dunhill pipe tobacco, Guinness, and Bulmer's Cider.

GENEALOGY AND FAMILY HISTORY
As the interest in family history and roots grows world-wide, more and more people are turning to Frith's photographs of Great Britain for images of the towns, villages and streets where their ancestors lived; and, of course, photographs of the churches and chapels where their ancestors were christened, married and buried are an essential part of every genealogy tree and family album.

FRITH PRODUCTS
All Frith photographs are available Framed or just as Mounted Prints and unmounted versions. These may be ordered from the address below. Other products available are - Calendars, Jigsaws, Canvas Prints, Mugs, Tea Towels, Tableware and local and prestige books.

THE INTERNET
Over several hundred thousand Frith photographs can be viewed and purchased on the internet through the Frith websites!

For more detailed information on Frith products, look at
www.francisfrith.com

See the complete list of Frith Books at: www.francisfrith.com
This web site is regularly updated with the latest list of publications from The Francis Frith Collection. If you wish to buy books relating to another part of the country that your local bookshop does not stock, you may purchase on-line.

For further information, trade, or author enquiries please contact us at the address below:
The Francis Frith Collection, Unit 19 Kingsmead Business Park, Gillingham, Dorset SP8 5FB.
Tel: +44 (0)1722 716 376   Email: sales@francisfrith.co.uk

See Frith products on the internet at www.francisfrith.com

FREE PRINT OF YOUR CHOICE
CHOOSE A PHOTOGRAPH FROM THIS BOOK
+ POSTAGE

Mounted Print
Overall size 14 x 11 inches (355 x 280mm)

TO RECEIVE YOUR FREE PRINT

Choose any Frith photograph in this book
Simply complete the Voucher opposite and return it with your payment (to cover postage and handling) and we will print the photograph of your choice in SEPIA (size 11 x 8 inches) and supply it in a cream mount ready to frame (overall size 14 x 11 inches).

Order additional Mounted Prints at HALF PRICE - £19.00 each (normally £38.00)
If you would like to order more Frith prints from this book, possibly as gifts for friends and family, you can buy them at half price (with no additional postage costs).

Have your Mounted Prints framed
For an extra £20.00 per print you can have your mounted print(s) framed in an elegant polished wood and gilt moulding, overall size 16 x 13 inches (no additional postage required).

IMPORTANT!

❶ Please note: aerial photographs and photographs with a reference number starting with a "Z" are not Frith photographs and cannot be supplied under this offer.

❷ Offer valid for delivery to one UK address only.

❸ These special prices are only available if you use this form to order. You must use the ORIGINAL VOUCHER on this page (no copies permitted). We can only despatch to one UK address.

❹ This offer cannot be combined with any other offer.

As a customer your name & address will be stored by Frith but not sold or rented to third parties. Your data will be used for the purpose of this promotion only.

Send completed Voucher form to:
The Francis Frith Collection,
1 Chilmark Estate House, Chilmark,
Salisbury, Wiltshire SP3 5DU

Voucher for FREE and Reduced Price Frith Prints

Please do not photocopy this voucher. Only the original is valid, so please fill it in, cut it out and return it to us with your order.

Picture ref no	Page no	Qty	Mounted @ £19.00	Framed + £20.00	Total Cost £
		1	Free of charge*	£	£
			£19.00	£	£
			£19.00	£	£
			£19.00	£	£
			£19.00	£	£

Please allow 28 days for delivery. Offer available to one UK address only

* Post & handling	£3.80
Total Order Cost	£

Title of this book ....

I enclose a cheque/postal order for £ ....

made payable to 'Heritage Resource Management Ltd'

OR please debit my Mastercard / Visa / Maestro card, details below

Card Number:

Issue No (Maestro only):   Valid from (Maestro):

Card Security Number: Expires:

Signature:

Name Mr/Mrs/Ms ....

Address ....

....

....

.... Postcode ....

Daytime Tel No ....

Email ....

Valid to 31/12/26

Free Print – see overleaf

Can you help us with information about any of the Frith photographs in this book?

We are gradually compiling an historical record for each of the photographs in the Frith archive. It is always fascinating to find out the names of the people shown in the pictures, as well as insights into the shops, buildings and other features depicted.

If you recognize anyone in the photographs in this book, or if you have information not already included in the author's caption, do let us know. We would love to hear from you, and will try to publish it in future books or articles.

An Invitation from The Francis Frith Collection to Share Your Memories

The 'Share Your Memories' feature of our website allows members of the public to add personal memories relating to the places featured in our photographs, or comment on others already added. Seeing a place from your past can rekindle forgotten or long held memories. Why not visit the website, find photographs of places you know well and add YOUR story for others to read and enjoy? We would love to hear from you!

www.francisfrith.com/memories

Our production team

Frith books are produced by a small dedicated team at offices near Salisbury. Most have worked with the Frith Collection for many years. All have in common one quality: they have a passion for the Frith Collection.

Frith Books and Gifts

We have a wide range of books and gifts available on our website utilising our photographic archive, many of which can be individually personalised.

www.francisfrith.com